SARAH LAUGHED:
Sonnets from Genesis

Judith Goodbode

SARAH LAUGHED:
Sonnets from Genesis

By Judith Goldhaber

Illustrations by Gerson Goldhaber

RIBBONWEED PRESS
BERKELEY, CALIFORNIA

SARAH LAUGHED:
Sonnets from Genesis

Published by
Ribbonweed Press
Berkeley, California
www.ribbonweedpress.com

SARAH LAUGHED: Sonnets from Genesis
© 2007 by Judith & Gerson Goldhaber
First Edition 2007

ISBN-13: 978-0-9761554-1-6
ISBN-10: 0-9761554-1-9
Library of Congress Control Number: 2006940315

Cover art: Gerson Goldhaber
Cover design: Dianna LaFerry
Layout & Typesetting: Lazer Image

Printed by Regal Printing Ltd., Hong Kong
Printed in China

For our parents

Berthe & Harry Margoshes

and

Ethel & Charles Goldhaber

the storytellers

ALSO BY JUDITH & GERSON GOLDHABER

SONNETS FROM AESOP

Winner of the Independent Publisher
"Outstanding Book of the Year" Award

TABLE OF CONTENTS

2   EVE'S RIVAL

    i. The Other Wife

    ii. We Were Happy

    iii. Deep in Love

    iv. You Know About the Snake

    v. Was She Fair?

    vi. A Better Plan

    vii. We Must Not Eat that Fruit

    viii. An Awful Flap

    ix. Getting Acquainted

22   THE IGNORANCE OF CAIN

    i. The Ignorance of Cain

26   NOAH AND THE FLOOD

    i. A Day of Pouring Rain

    ii. The Time is Coming

    iii. The Laughing Stock

    iv. Bird to Bird

    v. A Mighty Cry

vi.   The Lights Go Out

vii.   Howling for their Meals

viii.   A Bite of Juicy Steer

ix.   The Lion and the Lamb

x.   Tikkun

xi.   The Olive Branch

xii.   The World's Rebirth

52   THE TOWER OF BABEL

i.   Bricks and Mortar

ii.   Scorn for Human Life

iii.   A Nasty Trick

iv.   A Babble of Strange Sound

62   ABRAHAM THE WANDERER

i.   The Sojourn in Haran

ii.   The Journey

iii.   Canaan

iv.   At Pharaoh's Throne

v.   Sarah and the Pharaoh

vi.   Home Again

vii.   God Rebukes Abraham

78   ABRAHAM AND HIS TWO SONS

    i. A Twist of Fate

    ii. A Heavy Price

    iii. The Well in the Desert

    iv. Sarah Laughed

    v. The Final Test

    vi. The Sacrifice

    vii. What's Still to Come

94   THE DEATH OF ABRAHAM

    i. The Angel's Plea

    ii. The Last Wish

    iii. The Promised Land

102   JACOB AND THE ANGEL

    i. In Silent Struggle

    ii. The Quiet Man

    iii. Mislead, Betray

    iv. Dreams and Visions

    v. No Second Chance

    vi. An Angel's Intervention

    vii. Into the Fire

    viii. The End of Days

120   JOSEPH AND HIS BROTHERS

    i. For Joseph's Sake

    ii. The Dreamer Cometh

    iii. A Fine Young Man

    iv. Never to Reveal

    v. Jacob and the Wolf

    vi. The Words of the Wolf

    vii. The Cruel Secret

    viii. Meanwhile in Egypt

138   THE REUNION

    i. The Ten Brothers

    ii. The Youngest Brother

    iii. The Souvenir

    iv. Bad News

    v. A Day of Celebration

    vi. That Old Man

    vii. Proof of Robbery

    viii. One Last Chance

    ix. Come Closer

    x. Sudden Joy

    xi. The Sound of Music

    xii. Serah's Song

    xiii. Shalom!

    xiv. Visions of the Night

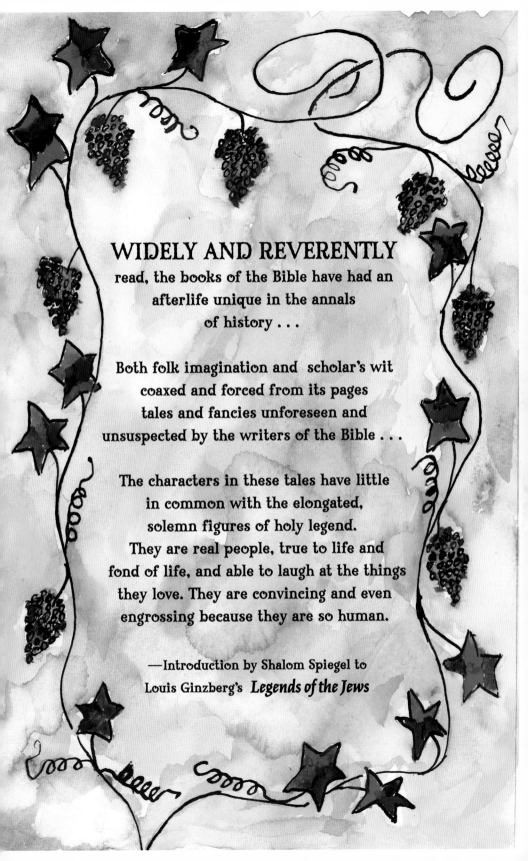

WIDELY AND REVERENTLY
read, the books of the Bible have had an
afterlife unique in the annals
of history . . .

Both folk imagination and scholar's wit
coaxed and forced from its pages
tales and fancies unforeseen and
unsuspected by the writers of the Bible . . .

The characters in these tales have little
in common with the elongated,
solemn figures of holy legend.
They are real people, true to life and
fond of life, and able to laugh at the things
they love. They are convincing and even
engrossing because they are so human.

—Introduction by Shalom Spiegel to
Louis Ginzberg's *Legends of the Jews*

EVE'S RIVAL

GENESIS gives two accounts
of the creation of humans. In the
first (Genesis 1:27), man and woman
are created at the same time, from the dust
of the earth:
"AND GOD CREATED man in His own
image, in the image of God created He
him; male and female created He them."

IN THE SECOND (Genesis 2:18),
woman is created later, from Adam's
rib: AND GOD SAID: "It is not good
that the man should be alone; I
will make him a help
meet for him." . . .

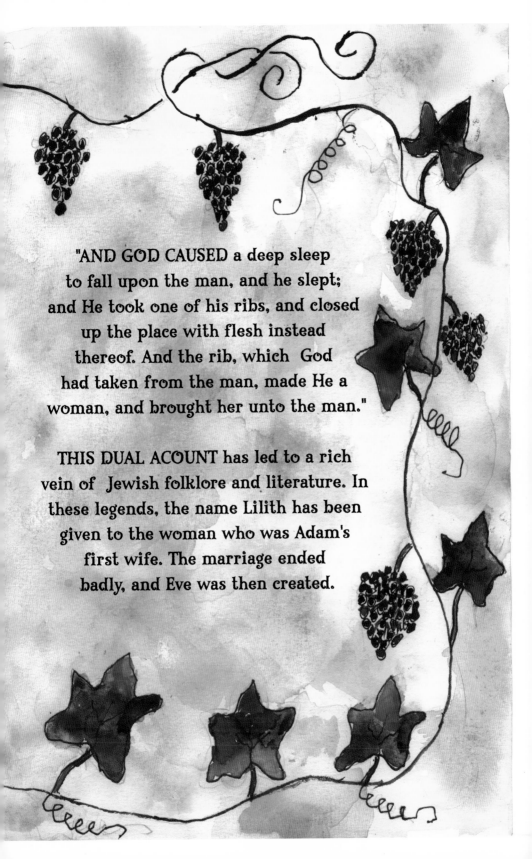

"AND GOD CAUSED a deep sleep
to fall upon the man, and he slept;
and He took one of his ribs, and closed
up the place with flesh instead
thereof. And the rib, which God
had taken from the man, made He a
woman, and brought her unto the man."

THIS DUAL ACOUNT has led to a rich
vein of Jewish folklore and literature. In
these legends, the name Lilith has been
given to the woman who was Adam's
first wife. The marriage ended
badly, and Eve was then created.

EVE'S RIVAL

i. The "Other Wife"

At first I thought that Lilith was all wrong —
claiming to be his peer in every way,
fashioned, just like him, from dust and clay
and just as wise, autonomous, and strong.
For these beliefs, she'd been pronounced headstrong
and disobedient, so she ran away.
Angels gave chase and ordered her to stay
with Adam, but she shrugged, "We don't belong
together; better we should live apart.
To tell the truth, I never felt at home
in Eden. Let him make a brand new start."
With that she vanished in the Red Sea's foam.
Now, I had heard this story all my life
and often thought about that "other wife."

EVE'S RIVAL

ii. We Were Happy

I often thought about that other wife,
and so I was determined to be good,
to win the praise of all the neighborhood
avoiding all the rivalry and strife
with which that youthful marriage had been rife.
I sought to please in every way I could,
and never gave a clue to how I stood
on matters of importance in our life.
The naming of the animals, for one —
Some of his choices were ridiculous:
Honestly, folks, a hippopotamus?
and yet I kept the peace, and held my tongue,
making our bower a harmonious shrine.
So we were happy, everything was fine.

EVE'S RIVAL

iii. Deep in Love

We were happy, everything was fine;
I loved him dearly, and it was enough
to share the garden and the fruits thereof.
The garden yielded honey, figs, and wine;
our marriage bed swung from a flowering vine,
angels served us with the finest stuff,
and don't forget that I was deep in love,
and Adam's face and figure were divine!
In later generations, some men tried
to match their father in his strength and grace:
Samson possessed his strength, and Saul his face,
Absalom his hair, and yet, beside
my husband, fashioned in the Lord's own shape,
each of them seemed no better than an ape.

EVE'S RIVAL

iv. You Know About the Snake

So why, you ask, did I commit the sin
I'm famous for? You know about the snake
and how all mankind suffers for my sake,
but over centuries the facts have been
somewhat distorted, so let us begin
at the beginning. Once as I lay awake
while Adam slept, a sudden knife-edged ache
tore my heart open, and let the serpent in.
"Lilith!" I wondered, "Does he ever dream
of her? Was she more beautiful than I?
They say she dumped him, but they don't say why."
And so that night I hatched a little scheme
to learn the truth about this mystery
at any cost. The rest is history.

EVE'S RIVAL

v. Was She Fair?

"Sir Serpent," I began, "I know you're wise,
wiser than all the creatures in the garden,
and so I need you now to take my part in
an awkward matter. I beg you to advise
me honestly, not flatter me with lies
or turn away contemptuously and harden
your heart, for though the Lord may never pardon
my impudence, I've come to realize
I need to understand a whole lot more
about this woman, Lilith. You were there,
Sir Serpent, tell me truly, was she fair?
fairer than I? And *he* — did he adore
her? And what happened when she left?
Did he tear out all his hair and seem bereft?"

EVE'S RIVAL

vi. A Better Plan

"Ah," sighed the snake, "I'd help you if I could,
victims always get my sympathy,
and I'm most honored that you came to me
for guidance. Yes, I really think you should
know the whole truth, but it would do no good
for me to tell. A better plan would be
to taste the fruit that grows upon the tree
that's planted in the middle of our wood.
I hear that once you've eaten of that fruit
you're privy to the scandalous details
of anybody's life. It never fails!
And once you know the truth, you can refute
the gossip-mongers, and yourself decide
if Eve or Lilith is his rightful bride."

EVE'S RIVAL

vii. We Must Not Eat that Fruit

"Serpent," I answered, "Thanks for your advice,
but just the same I'm going to resist
temptation. God and Adam both insist
we must not eat that fruit — indeed, the price
is high: they'd boot us out of Paradise."
"Ah! Lilith would have tasted it," he hissed,
"and later she and Adam would have kissed,
her mouth delectable with fragrant spice,
his soft tongue lapping up the juice that drips
over her chin and breasts, so he could share
her boldness and her sin. Yes, he would dare
God's wrath to drink that honey from her lips.
But, Eve, don't worry, *'chaque un à son gout';*
I guess such escapades are not for you."

EVE'S RIVAL

viii. An Awful Flap

You know the rest. I fell into the trap.
The fruit was spiny, underripe, and sour,
not the sort of thing you would devour
for pleasure. Then there was an awful flap
and in the end I had to take the rap
for mankind's falling into Satan's power.
I had a stomach-ache within the hour
and finally lost my lunch on Adam's lap.
But in the end, of course, we reconciled;
the marriage, now, is built on firmer ground,
and Adam — well, the times he is around,
no longer treats me like a wayward child.
Of course he's working hard to earn our bread
through sweat and labor, as the good Lord said.

EVE'S RIVAL

ix. Getting Acquainted

And, best of all, when we were settled here
Lilith came by — at last we got acquainted!
When she walked in I swear I almost fainted!
She's headstrong, yes, but absolutely clear
in what she wants, so I have naught to fear
from her. She's not as bad as she's been painted —
neither of us is likely to be sainted
but we have lots in common, it appears.
We get together sometimes, reminisce
about the days we spent in Paradise —
we were so young, and none of us were wise —
we were not ready for a life of bliss.
But now we're older, and I think there's room
for both of us to lie in Adam's tomb.

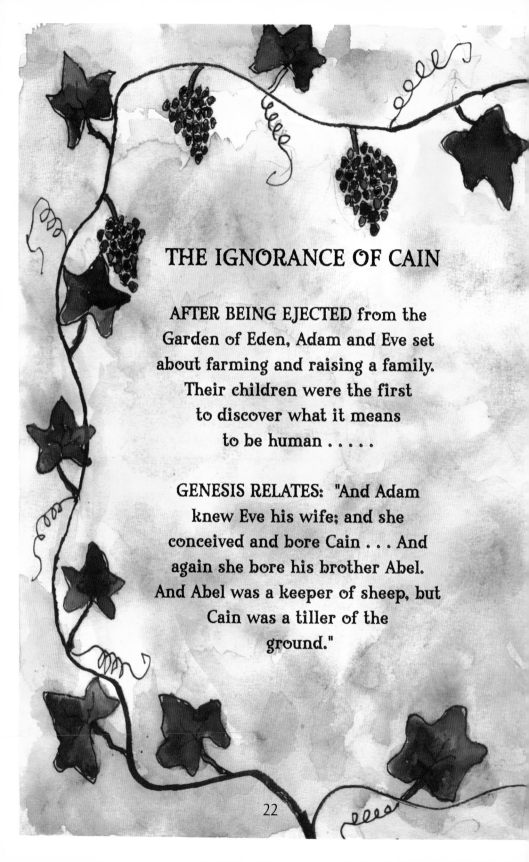

THE IGNORANCE OF CAIN

AFTER BEING EJECTED from the
Garden of Eden, Adam and Eve set
about farming and raising a family.
Their children were the first
to discover what it means
to be human . . . . .

GENESIS RELATES: "And Adam
knew Eve his wife; and she
conceived and bore Cain . . . And
again she bore his brother Abel.
And Abel was a keeper of sheep, but
Cain was a tiller of the
ground."

"And . . . Cain brought of the fruit
of the ground an offering to God.
And Abel also brought of the
firstborn of his flock . . . And
God had respect unto Abel
and to his offering; but unto Cain
and to his offering He had not respect.
And Cain was very wroth,
and his countenance fell."

". . . And it came to pass, when they were
in the field, that Cain rose up
against Abel his brother, and
slew him." (Genesis 4:1–8)

THE IGNORANCE
OF CAIN

Ignorance of the law is no excuse
you say, but picture yourself in my place —
the firstborn offspring of the human race,
guileless and raw and ignorant as a goose.
Why was I singled out to introduce
mankind to death and violence and disgrace?
When all that blood gushed from his wounded face
I blanched, and cried out, "Truce, my brother, truce!"
But Abel didn't answer. He looked the same
as usual, so I wiped the blood away
and watched it puddle on the sunbaked clay.
I propped him up and called him by his name,
blew in his ears and warmed him with my breath,
I never imagined such a thing as death.

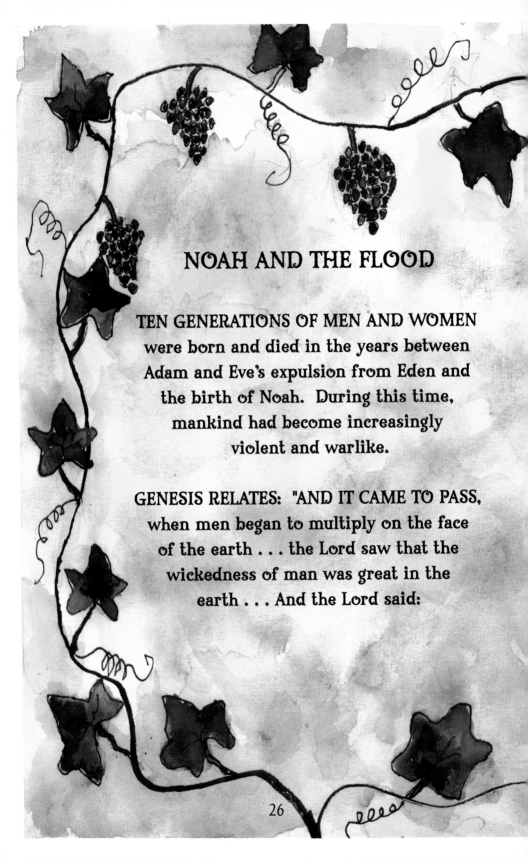

NOAH AND THE FLOOD

TEN GENERATIONS OF MEN AND WOMEN
were born and died in the years between
Adam and Eve's expulsion from Eden and
the birth of Noah. During this time,
mankind had become increasingly
violent and warlike.

GENESIS RELATES: "AND IT CAME TO PASS,
when men began to multiply on the face
of the earth . . . the Lord saw that the
wickedness of man was great in the
earth . . . And the Lord said:

26

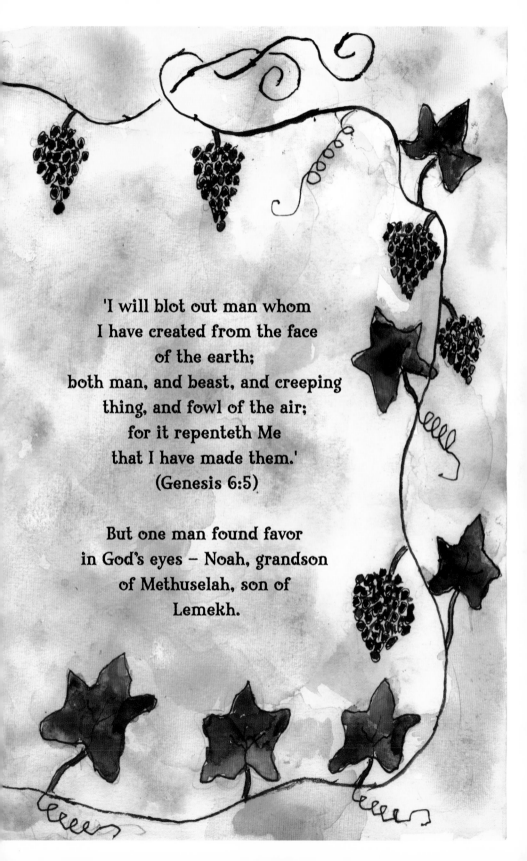

'I will blot out man whom
I have created from the face
of the earth;
both man, and beast, and creeping
thing, and fowl of the air;
for it repenteth Me
that I have made them.'
(Genesis 6:5)

But one man found favor
in God's eyes – Noah, grandson
of Methuselah, son of
Lemekh.

NOAH
AND THE FLOOD

i. A Day of Pouring Rain

The wicked sons and grandchildren of Cain
grew multitudinous, and defiled the earth
with idol worship and unseemly mirth
over the fallen bodies of their slain
enemies, regarding with disdain
censure from men of decency and worth.
And so corruption grew until the birth
of Noah, on a day of pouring rain.
The body of the babe was white as snow
and red as a blooming rose, his hair was white
and from his open eyes came beams of light
like sunshine, till the whole house seemed to glow.
The rain stopped, storm clouds scurried from the sky,
and Noah said, "Hineini, here am I."

NOAH
AND THE FLOOD

ii. The Time is Coming

God spoke to Noah when he became a man
and said, "The time is coming — build an Ark;
storm clouds are gathering; soon you will embark
upon the seas, as outlined in My plan.
Make the Ark as sturdy as you can —
line it with pitch, strip gopher trees of bark
to shape the hull, and lest it be too dark
cut windows, and a doorway." Noah began
to do what God commanded, but worked slowly,
hoping in time the Lord might change His mind
regarding the destruction of mankind.
He begged the wicked to return to holy
customs, but they answered him with jeers.
And thus went by one hundred twenty years.

NOAH
AND THE FLOOD

iii. The Laughing Stock

At last the Ark was finished, and it stood
three hundred cubits long, and fifty wide,
three stories — thirty cubits — high inside
constructed out of seasoned gopher wood,
the laughing stock of Noah's neighborhood.
"A flood?" the people mocked, *"I'm terrified!*
Look! Over there! Is that a rising tide
I see? Boo-hoo, I promise to be good!"
But then Methuselah died, and a malaise
descended on the people, for they knew
that God had stayed His hand until the few
good men still living reached their final days.
A dark cloud veiled the sun; the sky was bleak,
and Noah sniffed the wind and said, "A week."

NOAH
AND THE FLOOD

iv. Bird to Bird

Compared to getting humankind to heed
the urgent warnings, putting out the word
to animals was easy. Bird to bird
the news was spread at supersonic speed.
By nightfall all the beasts of earth had heard
the message, and they readily agreed
to group themselves according to their breed
(scaly, hairy, hard-shelled, feathered, furred)
and line up in a queue beside the Ark.
Birds sang and cattle mooed and lions roared
as Noah gently welcomed them aboard
and sealed the door against the growing dark.
At last, on bended knee, nose to the ground,
he gathered up the ants, lest they be drowned.

NOAH
AND THE FLOOD
v. A Mighty Cry

The sun turned black, and lightning streaked the sky,
somewhere behind the clouds a strange light bloomed
and faded, and at last the thunder boomed,
bringing the first drops. Then a mighty cry
arose from those who'd chosen to defy
the warning signs, and callously resumed
their sinful ways. "Even now you are not doomed,"
despairing, Noah cried, "repent or die!"
On board the Ark, through unbelieving eyes
the animals beheld the death of man.
Sworn adversaries since the world began
wept freely as they said their last goodbyes.
Even man's ancient enemy the snake
shed bitter tears that day for mankind's sake.

NOAH
AND THE FLOOD

vi. The Lights Go Out

It rained for forty days and forty nights;
the waters rose until they bore the Ark
above the mountains. When the last landmark
sank underwater and was lost to sight
the sun and moon and stars put out the light.
The vessel plunged and staggered in the dark.
Then even Noah, the righteous patriarch,
thinking that death was near, cried out in fright.
"Help us Lord! Death stares us in the face —
be gracious unto us! Redeem and save!"
"Earth's fate depends on how you men behave
from this time forth," said God. "Man can erase
his sinfulness by kindness to his brother.
Here on the Ark, take care of one another."

NOAH
AND THE FLOOD

vii. Howling for Their Meals

So Noah set about providing food
for all the beasts and coaxing them to try it.
There were transgressions: craving his old diet
of bugs, an aardvark hunted and pursued
and ate a termite, though all meat was tabooed.
As you might guess, this almost caused a riot.
Diurnal hunters as a rule were quiet —
darkness enfolded them in lassitude —
but the night prowlers — cats and skunks and owls —
were wide awake, and howling for their meals.
The Ark resounded with their loud appeals —
meows and hisses, screeches, squeals, and yowls.
Sighed Noah, in the galley, kneading bran,
"Patience, friends! I'm doing the best I can."

NOAH
AND THE FLOOD

viii. A Bite of Juicy Steer

Years later, Noah talked about the trouble
he had providing food for one full year
for all the animals. "Giraffes and deer
wanted green leaves, and didn't like the stubble
we had on board the Ark, and that went double
for carnivores, who thought me too severe,
denying them a bite of juicy steer.
Sex also was forbidden, though a couple
of animals — rabbits, for instance — sinned
in that regard as often as they could.
I tried my best to keep the creatures good
and warm and clean and fed and disciplined,
because the Lord had shown me the true worth
of every soul that creepeth on the earth."

NOAH
AND THE FLOOD

ix. The Lion and the Lamb

One day he found a lion fast asleep
beside a lamb. "Friend, have you food to eat?"
he asked the lion. "I'm fine! Please have a seat,"
the lion replied. "I don't see how you keep
it up — the way you cook, and clean, and sweep!
In fact, it seems you're always on your feet!
Sure I'm hungry, but I won't compete
with creatures who are needier, like this sheep."
The flood prevailed a hundred and fifty days,
till every living thing on earth was gone,
but on the Ark a strange phenomenon
had taken place among the castaways.
The day the lion and lamb lay down together
God smiled and said, "It's time to change the weather."

NOAH
AND THE FLOOD

x. Tikkun

The sages say that it was Noah's love
for all the creatures given to his care
that brought about *tikkun*, divine repair
of all our sinning world. The waters of
the flood began to ebb, and high above
the waterline a rainbow arc'd the air.
Between the clouds the sun rose like a prayer
and into that radiance Noah launched a dove.
Twice he sent her forth, a week apart.
She circled the globe but, finding no dry land,
returned to Noah, who put forth his hand
and held her, mourning, close against his heart.
"You must be tired, child, don't be distressed,"
he said, smoothing her feathers, "go and rest."

NOAH
AND THE FLOOD

xi. The Olive Branch

Once more he sent her forth; on the third week
she flew back to the Ark at eventide,
holding an olive branch within her beak.
"Father, I have traveled far and wide,
and I have found the very thing you seek
growing in the hilly countryside
eastward of Eden. I will be your guide
to where it grows, atop a mountain peak."
The first of Tishri was the actual date
(if what the rabbis calculate is true)
that Noah's Ark with all its precious freight
of mankind and God's creatures, two by two,
and all the generations they begat
came to rest at last on Ararat.

NOAH
AND THE FLOOD

xii. The World's Rebirth

Then every beast, and every creeping thing
and every fowl that moved upon the earth
went forth to celebrate the world's rebirth
while Noah tendered a burnt offering
and birds high in the trees began to sing
so that the planet rang with joy and mirth.
The rainbow grew, encircling in its girth
the whole healed world, in all its blossoming.
Impatient to obey the Lord's command
to go forth in the earth and multiply,
the creatures hastened out across the land.
But Noah sat alone and watched the sky
turn dark, until one star appeared, and soon
rising over Ararat, the moon.

THE TOWER OF BABEL

AFTER THE FLOOD, the nations spread abroad on the earth. Genesis tells us "And the whole earth was of one language and of one speech . . ."

As the people migrated from the east, they found a valley in the land of Shinar, and they settled there.

THEY SAID TO ONE ANOTHER,
"Come, let us mold bricks
and fire them." They then
had bricks to use as stone, and
asphalt for mortar.

They said, "Come, let us build
ourselves a city, and a tower
whose top shall reach
the sky. Let us make ourselves
a name, so that we will not
be scattered all over
the face of the earth." (Genesis 11)

THE TOWER OF BABEL

i. Bricks and Mortar

Back in the days of haughty Nimrod's rule
the earth was of one language and one speech,
and nothing seemed beyond a mortal's reach
if he had bricks, and mortar, and a tool.
"Come, let us build a tower," said a fool,
"so men can climb to Paradise, and breach
heaven's gate, and strike it down, and teach
God himself the sting of ridicule."
The tower they built in Shinar rose so high
it took a year to clamber to the top.
Not a single brick did they let drop,
but no one raised a murmur or outcry
if a man or woman plummeted to earth,
since human life was deemed of little worth.

THE TOWER OF BABEL

ii. Scorn for Human Life

At first God merely smiled at men's presumption.
He had created them to be ambitious
and didn't view their efforts as seditious
but merely an expression of the gumption
He liked to see in them. But that assumption
soon changed. "This scorn for human life is vicious,"
quoth He, "an intervention is propitious
if humankind will ever find redemption.
Let us go down to earth and move among
mortals," He told his angels, "I have a plan
to put a stop to all these schemes of man."
And so it came to pass that each man's tongue
was twisted so that when he tried to talk
to other men, it sounded like a squawk.

THE TOWER OF BABEL

iii. A Nasty Trick

"Hand me that hammer, please," one man might say,
and when his neighbor handed him a brick
instead, he thought it was a nasty trick
and threw it at him. No one could convey
the simplest thought: Hebrew's "yea," or "nay"
might mean the opposite in Arabic,
and if you tried to buy a candlestick
you might bring home a fish, to your dismay.
Soon mankind scattered all around the globe
and settled down at various locations
and joined together to establish nations.
Soon after that, the world's first xenophobe
(incited by the first provocateur)
came up with mankind's greatest evil, war.

THE TOWER OF BABEL

iv. A Babble of Strange Sound

As for the tower, it sank into the ground;
its turrets shattered and consumed by fire;
just one remains, a symbol of the ire
of God, and of his power to confound
man's language to a babble of strange sound.
Whoever passes by the lonely spire
rising from the desolate quagmire
that once was Shinar, stops and stares, spellbound,
and in the shadow of that minaret
all that he ever held in memory,
the clamor of the world's cacophony
is wiped away, along with all regret,
and in its place he hears the harmony
of how things were, and how they still could be.

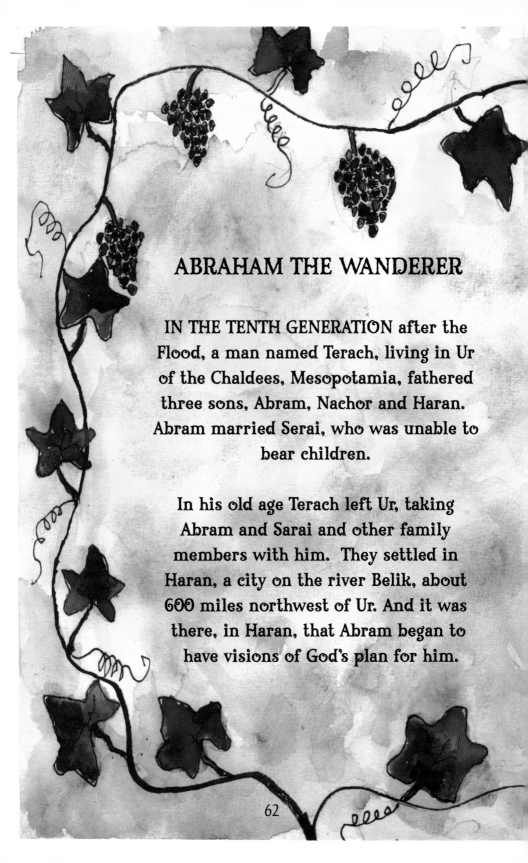

ABRAHAM THE WANDERER

IN THE TENTH GENERATION after the Flood, a man named Terach, living in Ur of the Chaldees, Mesopotamia, fathered three sons, Abram, Nachor and Haran. Abram married Serai, who was unable to bear children.

In his old age Terach left Ur, taking Abram and Sarai and other family members with him. They settled in Haran, a city on the river Belik, about 600 miles northwest of Ur. And it was there, in Haran, that Abram began to have visions of God's plan for him.

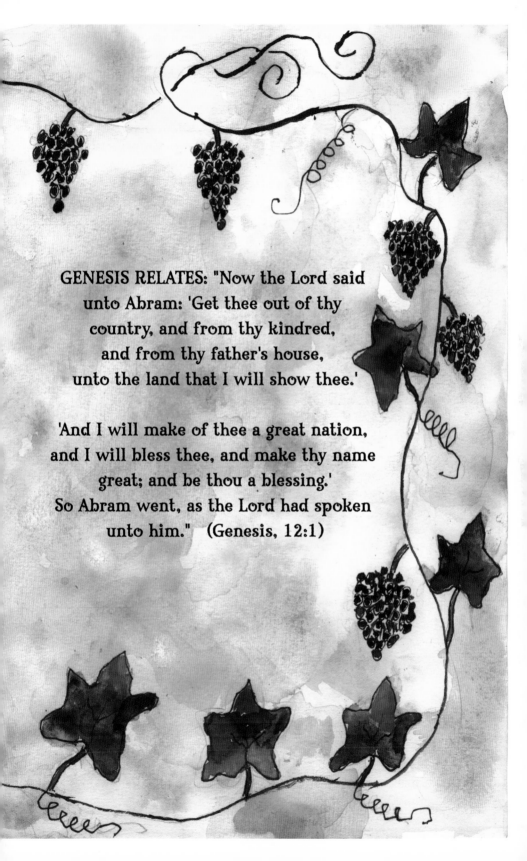

GENESIS RELATES: "Now the Lord said
unto Abram: 'Get thee out of thy
country, and from thy kindred,
and from thy father's house,
unto the land that I will show thee.'

'And I will make of thee a great nation,
and I will bless thee, and make thy name
great; and be thou a blessing.'
So Abram went, as the Lord had spoken
unto him."   (Genesis, 12:1)

ABRAHAM
THE WANDERER

i. The Sojourn in Haran

At first it seemed a pretty good idea,
quitting our ancient home near Babylon
and moving the whole *mishpoche* to Haran.
The moon god, Sin, whom local folk revere
seemed less degenerate than Nimrod's queer
and arrogant wizards, with their pantheon
of serpents, birds and chimeras — the spawn
of dying gods. And once we'd settled there
I found the market town a pleasant place
and hoped to settle into village life —
a new beginning for my sad-eyed wife
whose barren womb had brought her such disgrace.
But in my dreams we trudged through desert sand,
barefoot and starving, towards some promised land.

ABRAHAM
THE WANDERER

ii. The Journey

The visions never showed the destination,
only the journey, so we never knew
if we'd arrived where we were going to.
In Aram-naharaim, a small way station
on the Euphrates, a second revelation
was given me, and I believed it true:
God said to me "Abram, I've chosen you;
from you I plan to make a mighty nation."
I looked around, and asked "Is this the place?
the promised land of which my visions spoke?
You may have noticed that the local folk
are idol worshippers, a wanton race.
I'll gladly go wherever You command
but please don't leave me in this godless land."

ABRAHAM
THE WANDERER

iii. Canaan

And so we traveled on from town to town,
footsore and weary, waiting for a sign
that we had reached the land that would be mine.
We stopped to rest in Canaan at sundown;
the sun was setting like a golden crown
on cultivated fields and fruitful vines.
In my heart I hoped God would assign
this place to me, this charmed and blessed ground.
But I was a stranger in the promised land
and soon those fruitful vines, those fields of grain
wilted and shriveled up for lack of rain,
shuddering under famine's heavy hand.
To Canaan then we said a sad goodbye
and traveled on again, Sarah and I.

ABRAHAM
THE WANDERER

iv. At Pharaoh's Throne

Now, Sarah was as beautiful as a dove
ascending with the sunrise on its wings,
her voice melodious as the lark that sings
in rapture as it tumbles from above
the clouds to skim the shining surface of
the earth below. In all our wanderings
shepherds and philosophers and kings
took one look at her and fell in love.
What were we to do? In desperation
lest men should kill me for her beauty's sake
we made a rather serious mistake
and fibbed a bit about our true relation.
At Pharaoh's throne I swore she was my sister
and stood by silently as Pharaoh kissed her.

ABRAHAM
THE WANDERER

v. Sarah and the Pharaoh

That night, when Pharaoh took her to his bed
an angel showed up, carrying a rod
and a stern memorandum sent by God
not to touch a hair on Sarah's head
but to bow down and honor her instead.
All through the night the angel mounted guard
over Sarah, poking with his sharp prod
Pharaoh, the disgruntled newlywed.
At dawn a sleepless Pharaoh summoned me.
"What's going on?" he asked. "What did I do?
The moment that I touched your sister's shoe
all hell broke loose," he scowled. "Who is she?"
"I'm sorry," I confessed, "she is my wife,
we only lied to you to save my life."

ABRAHAM
THE WANDERER

vi. Home Again

"Go on your way!" said Pharaoh. "Take some gold!
How about a diamond? Please, take two!
You'll need some sheep and oxen, and a few
strong camels, too, the choicest of the fold,
and bushels of grain, all that your wagons hold!"
Then Pharaoh, flanked by all his retinue,
called after us until we passed from view
"I meant no insult! Blame the lies you told!"
We came again to Canaan in the spring.
Three months had passed. We built an altar there
and hallowed it with many a fervent prayer
to give thanks for our joyful homecoming.
I loved my wife, and I was reconciled
to going to my grave without a child.

ABRAHAM
THE WANDERER

vii. God Rebukes Abraham

" In fact," I told the Lord, "I'm not so sure
I want a child, since You appear inclined
to punish poor bewildered humankind
from time to time with famine, flood, and war,
not to mention pestilence. What's more,
I read the stars, and they are so aligned
to mean that Abraham will leave behind
no children — just the covenant we swore."
"Abraham my son," the Lord replied
"stick to religion and philosophy —
put no reliance on astrology.
I and I alone your fate decide.
The stars will line up as I tell them to,
and there is nothing that I cannot do."

ABRAHAM AND HIS TWO SONS

RETURNING LADEN WITH GIFTS
after their sojourn in Egypt, Abraham
and Sarah settled down in Canaan,
where they had first raised an altar
to God.

Abraham was a respected and
contented man, resigned to his one
secret sorrow – that his beloved wife
Sarah was childless. That, however,
was about to change . . .

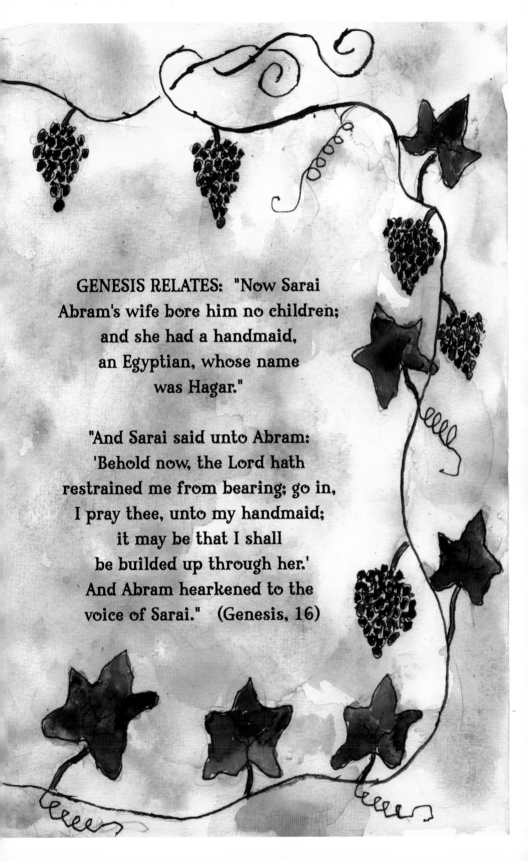

GENESIS RELATES: "Now Sarai
Abram's wife bore him no children;
and she had a handmaid,
an Egyptian, whose name
was Hagar."

"And Sarai said unto Abram:
'Behold now, the Lord hath
restrained me from bearing; go in,
I pray thee, unto my handmaid;
it may be that I shall
be builded up through her.'
And Abram hearkened to the
voice of Sarai." (Genesis, 16)

ABRAHAM
AND HIS TWO SONS

i. A Twist of Fate

For many years, Sarah and she were friends —
mistress and handmaiden, but nonetheless
companions who were known to share a dress,
make-up, and gossip. Sarah could comprehend
only too well the twist of fate that sends
one woman into exile and distress
while heaping another with the world's largesse.
In her own way, she sought to make amends.
"Please don't say a word until I'm through,"
Sarah said to me. "Abram, I fear
I'll never have a child to be your heir,
so this is what I think that we should do.
My maidservant is young — take her to bed
that you may have a child by her instead."

ABRAHAM
AND HIS TWO SONS

ii. A Heavy Price

Woe is me, I followed her advice.
Perhaps if I'd been able to foresee
the pain this choice would bring to her and me
and to our poor maidservant, I'd think twice
and realize there would be a heavy price
for our desire for posterity.
For Sarah was consumed by jealousy
and demanded that I make a sacrifice
of Ishmael, the son that Hagar bore.
Twice I've been asked to sacrifice a son —
first by Sarah, then by the Holy One
Himself. Although it hurt me to the core
each time I bowed my head and acquiesced —
yet each time matters turned out for the best.

ABRAHAM
AND HIS TWO SONS

iii. The Well in the Desert

"What aileth thee?" the angel of the Lord
asked Hagar as she choked on desert sand.
"Arise, lift up your son, and hold his hand,
weep no more for Ishmael. Be assured
he shall not perish, but shall be restored
to you, for truly it is God's command
that he, and you, shall prosper in this land.
Open your eyes, and see your just reward."
She looked around in wonder and dismay
and saw a well of water at her feet;
the water there was pure, and fresh, and sweet,
and cool as moonlight in the heat of day.
Thus God reached forth His hand, and from the brink
pulled Hagar back, and gave her child a drink.

ABRAHAM
AND HIS TWO SONS

iv. Sarah Laughed

Sarah laughed when angels brought the news
that God would bless her ninety-year-old womb.
Then she denied the laugh, and I assume
it was that contradiction that amused
the Holy One Himself, and made Him choose
Isaac as the butt of jokes, on whom
God's tricks are played. Enroute to certain doom
on Mount Moriah, he'd said his last adieus —
but then an angel intervened. Not funny!
His own son Jacob tricked him as he lay
half-blind upon a couch, and stole away
the blessing, Esau's birthright, and the money.
And yet they call him "loved by God," and "blessed";
God must enjoy a joke, as Sarah guessed.

ABRAHAM
AND HIS TWO SONS

v. The Final Test

"Old man," God said, "you've done okay so far,
you've executed all I asked you to.
Without a backward glance you bade adieu
to Babylon. . . you challenged the bizarre
idols of Nimrod, chose treaties over war,
and cared for Canaan's fields. Of course it's true
I had to bail you out on quite a few
occasions, but now I see you are
as steadfast as a rock. What could I ask
of you, one final test in your old age
that might reveal a hidden streak of rage
against My rule? This is your final task:
take Isaac, thy beloved son, and bring
him to My altar as an offering."

ABRAHAM
AND HIS TWO SONS

vi. The Sacrifice

Three days we traveled to the chosen place,
leading a donkey piled with firewood,
and when at last we reached the neighborhood
of Mount Moriah, I stopped and turned my face
towards heaven. From Moriah's rocky base
we climbed a dizzying trail, until we stood
shrouded in sunset clouds, crimson as blood.
I folded Isaac in a last embrace
and made the altar ready, but the voice
of God Himself spoke from a pillar of fire,
"Abraham, stay your hand! I don't require
blood sacrifice from you — simply the choice
to follow where I lead, and do My will;
henceforward in My name thou shalt not kill.

ABRAHAM
AND HIS TWO SONS

vii. What's Still to Come

And so my wanderings ended; I've grown old,
my sons are grown and go their separate ways —
Ishmael is a hunter, spends his days
off in the forest, sleeps out in the cold,
I see him seldom; Isaac, though, I hold
close to my heart. At Sarah's burial place —
the cave where Eve and Adam still embrace
in death — we wept together, and consoled
each other's grief. *What's still to come?* I wonder.
God has been silent now for many years
though *I* still talk to *Him*. And if He hears
will He speak to me again out of the thunder?
Call my name, O Lord, and I'll reply
as in the past, "Hineini, here am I."

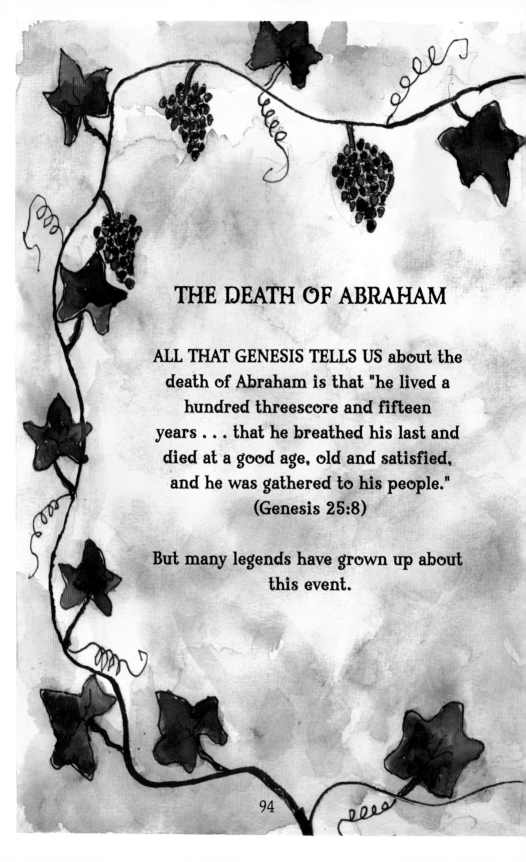

THE DEATH OF ABRAHAM

ALL THAT GENESIS TELLS US about the
death of Abraham is that "he lived a
hundred threescore and fifteen
years . . . that he breathed his last and
died at a good age, old and satisfied,
and he was gathered to his people."
(Genesis 25:8)

But many legends have grown up about
this event.

IN ONE STORY, when the
Angel of Death comes for him,
Abraham refuses to die
until one last wish
is granted him.

In another it is the Angel of
Death himself who cannot bear
to take Abraham's soul;
he weeps, and his tears fall
into a basin and
become precious stones . . .

THE DEATH
OF ABRAHAM

i. The Angel's Plea

In his one-hundred three-score fifteenth year
God sent an angel to gather Abraham's soul;
he entertained the angel unaware,
offering him drink, and lodging, and a bowl
of supper. When he kneeled to say a prayer
after the meal, the angel softly stole
away, and in a twinkling did appear
before God's throne. "Sire, I know my role
is to inform the righteous of their death
but, honestly, I've never seen a man
so kind, so pious since the world began —
I couldn't bear to take away his breath
in front of Isaac, his beloved son.
Please send somebody else, O Holy One!"

THE
DEATH OF ABRAHAM

ii. The Last Wish

"All men must die," said God, "but My old friend
Abraham, whose memory will inspire
generations of mankind to aspire
to seek, to strive, to find, and not to bend,
shall have one final wish before his end.
Go back to earth, My angel, and inquire
of his last wish and most profound desire.
Whatever he wishes, see that you attend."
And so the angel went down once again
to Abraham, and told him God's decree.
"I have been a wanderer among men
and traveled far, yet still I long to see
the whole of God's creation, earth and skies
and all his creatures spread before my eyes."

THE
DEATH OF ABRAHAM

iii. The Promised Land

"So shall it be," the angel said, and bowed
his head. Then sixty-seven cherubim
attended by a host of seraphim
lifted Abraham up to a cloud
from which all things on earth — both those allowed
and those forbidden — were revealed to him,
not seen as from afar, remote and dim,
but clearly, and the sounds of earth were loud
in Abraham's ears. He heard a baby's cry,
the rustle of leaves; he watched a beetle crawl
along a twig; then he felt his body fall
upward towards heaven, till he rose so high
the world grew smaller than a grain of sand,
and all around him lay the promised land.

JACOB AND THE ANGEL

ABRAHAM'S SON ISAAC was said to resemble his father in every way, and his children came late in his life, as they had for Abraham. He remained unmarried until the age of forty, and for 20 years after that, he and his wife, Rebecca, were childless.

But after the couple went together to Mount Moriah to pray for a child, Rebecca conceived.

Her pregnancy was difficult and full of pain, as if a bitter struggle was going on in her womb . . .

GENESIS RELATES: "And when her
days to be delivered were fulfilled,
behold, there were twins
in her womb.

And the first came forth ruddy,
all over like a hairy mantle;
and they called his name Esau.

And after that came forth his brother,
and his hand had hold on Esau's heel;
and his name was called Jacob."
(Genesis 25)

JACOB
AND THE ANGEL

i. In Silent Struggle

In silent struggle till the break of day,
lit only by the dying campfire's light
we wrestled through the watches of the night.
Chalk it up to pride or naiveté
I would not knuckle under and obey
this angel posing as a Canaanite—
crazy or drunk, and spoiling for a fight.
How could I guess his mission from Yahweh?
At dawn the angel pleaded "Let me go!"
"Not till you pay a ransom, sir!" said I.
Despite the pain and weakness in my thigh
I had him pinned down, helpless: "I must know
your business here, and from whence you came!"
He shook his head, and asked me for my name.

JACOB
AND THE ANGEL

ii. The Quiet Man

My name! The name that's haunted me since birth —
Jacob, *"usurper"* — think how *you* would feel,
born clinging tightly to your brother's heel
an object of resentment or of mirth
always measured against that brother's worth.
Quite soon I learned it wiser to conceal
my true identity, and offer up as real
this "quiet man," a tiller of the earth.
They learned the truth over a steaming plate
of lentils, hot and savory, served with bread
fresh from the oven; once he had been fed
Esau grew sulky, but by then it was too late.
For me, the die was cast, I knew my fate:
mislead, betray, pretend, manipulate.

JACOB
AND THE ANGEL

iii. Mislead, Betray

Mislead, betray, pretend, manipulate
became the way I made a path through life,
avoiding episodes of overt strife
in favor of juridical debate
intended to confuse and obfuscate.
When the time came for me to take a wife
I found that such shenanigans are rife
in families: my uncle made me wait
twice seven years to claim my chosen bride,
but I was patient, working out a scheme
involving cattle, spotted brown and cream,
and certain records changed and falsified
that put me back on top. And so I spent
my days on earth, conniving and content.

JACOB
AND THE ANGEL

iv. Dreams and Visions

I spent my *days* conniving and content,
but dreams and visions came to me at night.
Leaving Beer-sheba once, in hasty flight
from still another awkward incident
involving Esau, I stopped to pitch my tent
along the roadway at a barren site,
a stone my only pillow. Yet despite
this rocky bed, I fell asleep, and dreamt
of angels climbing on a golden stair!
It reached to heaven, up they climbed and down,
and on the top rung, with a golden crown
a blinding presence, who, it would appear
was God Himself! I woke then, full of fear,
and prayed for bread to eat and clothes to wear.

JACOB
AND THE ANGEL

v. No Second Chance

I prayed for bread to eat and clothes to wear,
and swore to seek my brother's hand in peace;
I vowed to serve God humbly, and to cease
the scandals that had marked my whole career.
Now, at the time I felt I was sincere,
but soon enough I'd found a way to fleece
my uncle on the matter of a lease
and arrange for certain lambs to disappear.
I thought sometimes of Beth-el, and the vow
I'd made to God, and of the golden rungs
and angels caroling in many tongues,
but man must function in the here and now;
I made my bed and chose my circumstance,
and surely there could be no second chance.

JACOB
AND THE ANGEL

vi. An Angel's Intervention

With no illusions of a second chance
and little in my life to recommend
an angel's intervention to defend
my life, I watched my enemies advance —
my uncle at the rear, with sword and lance,
the brother whom I'd hastened to offend
so many times, now waiting round the bend
with all his soldiers grouped in warlike stance.
We halted by the river Jabbock's shore;
I sent my wives and children on ahead
and waited there alone with mounting dread,
my pulses pounding with the drums of war,
when suddenly by the fire a stranger stood,
his body glistening like burnished wood.

JACOB
AND THE ANGEL

vii. Into the Fire

His burnished body glistened in the flame
the campfire cast; the air around him shone.
At last I said "I thought I was alone,"
thinking perhaps this silent envoy came
from Esau, or from Laban, with the aim
of compromise — a chance I could atone
for actions that I surely don't condone
in retrospect. I'd take on all the blame!
He spoke no word, but raised a shining arm
as if in greeting. "What do you desire?"
I boldly asked. He stepped into the fire.
After a frozen moment of alarm
and cowardice, I joined him in the flame,
knowing that things would never be the same.

JACOB
AND THE ANGEL

viii. The End of Days

Knowing that I would never be the same
after the night I wrestled face to face
with angel, god, or demon in that place
called Peniel, I cast away the shame
of Jacob's life, and with my newfound name
and fortitude, I recognized God's grace,
limping to meet my brother's warm embrace
(since, as you see, the struggle left me lame).
Though I am old now, living far from home
among an alien people and their gods,
their painted temples and their rich facades,
the angel's cry of "Israel, shalom!"
still summons me to glorify His ways
in silent struggle till the end of days.

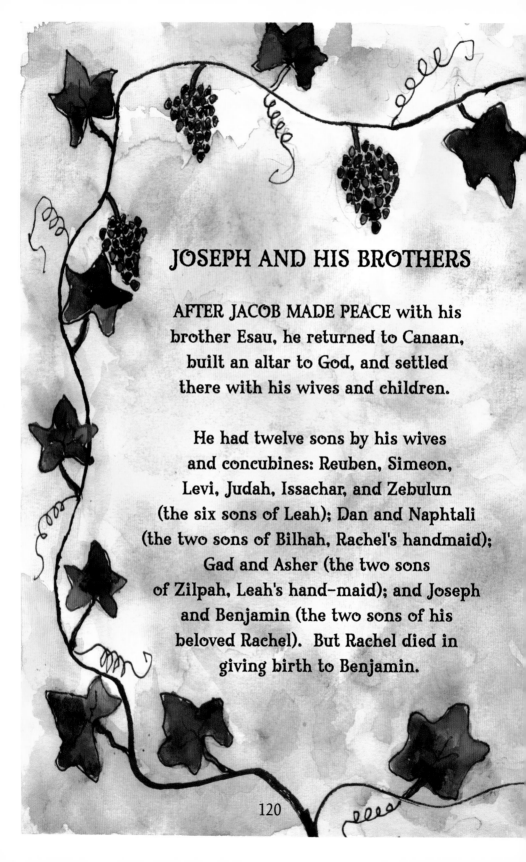

JOSEPH AND HIS BROTHERS

AFTER JACOB MADE PEACE with his brother Esau, he returned to Canaan, built an altar to God, and settled there with his wives and children.

He had twelve sons by his wives and concubines: Reuben, Simeon, Levi, Judah, Issachar, and Zebulun (the six sons of Leah); Dan and Naphtali (the two sons of Bilhah, Rachel's handmaid); Gad and Asher (the two sons of Zilpah, Leah's hand-maid); and Joseph and Benjamin (the two sons of his beloved Rachel). But Rachel died in giving birth to Benjamin.

GENESIS RELATES: "Now Jacob loved Joseph more than all his children, because he was the son of his old age; and he made him a coat of many colours."

"And when his brethren saw that their father loved him more than all his brethren, they hated him, and could not speak peaceably unto him." (Genesis, 37)

JOSEPH
AND HIS BROTHERS

i. For Joseph's Sake

His brothers called him sissy, tattletale,
they mocked his dreamy ways and mincing gait;
his powdered eyelids seemed to aggravate
their wrath, as did the painted fingernails,
the forehead curls and glossy oiled ducktail
of his hair. This built up into hate
by the time that he was seventeen — too late
for any truce, which would be doomed to fail.
The rainbow garment was the final straw —
this was the bone that stuck in Simon's craw —
Jacob among the women, spinning wool
and dyeing it to make it colorful,
and all for Joseph's sake, his pride and joy,
the son of his old age, his lovely boy.

JOSEPH
AND HIS BROTHERS

ii. The Dreamer Cometh

"Behold, the dreamer cometh," Simon said
to Levi, as they tended Jacob's flocks
in Dothan's pastures. "See the way he walks
scanning the heavens, with his head
up in the clouds as usual. I'm fed
up with him; his moony conduct mocks
our family, and makes us laughingstocks —
we'd all be better off if he were dead.
So let us slay him, toss him in a pit
and tell our father that some roaming beast,
a wolf or bear or tiger, made a feast
of him, and that's the end of it."
But Reuben told his brothers, "Shed no blood,
recall God's words to Noah at the Flood."

JOSEPH
AND HIS BROTHERS

iii. A Fine Young Man

Then Judah piped up, "Think, what will we gain
by killing him? A more resourceful plan
would be to sell him to a caravan
of Midianites en route to Egypt's plain.
Thus we get rid of him without the stain
of fratricide, which has disgraced our clan
ever since Cain slew Abel. A fine young man
like Joseph (with the beauty he's so vain
about) should surely fetch a fancy price
in Egypt, as a eunuch or a slave."
Twenty silver coins the Midianites gave
for Joseph, and they sold their merchandise
in Egypt's bustling slave-market bazaar
to Pharaoh's trusted captain, Potiphar.

JOSEPH
AND HIS BROTHERS

iv. Never to Reveal

Now Joseph's coat lay glimmering on the ground
where it had fallen when they stripped him bare.
Simon picked it up. "Now I will wear
this ostentatious rag; I'll say I found
it by the road as we were homeward bound."
"Madman," Reuben said, "you wouldn't dare!
Stop your rant and think! We all must swear
never to reveal, by sight or sound
to any mortal man what we have done,
and from this oath we'll never be released.
As for Joseph's garment, give it here!
We'll slay a young goat from the flock, and smear
the coat with blood. Jacob will think his son
was torn to pieces by a savage beast."

JOSEPH
AND HIS BROTHERS

v. Jacob and the Wolf

In the first raging torrent of his grief
his thoughts as sanguinary as that coat
smeared red with blood (we know now!) of a goat,
Jacob hoped revenge would bring relief
and told his sons, "Go forth and find the thief
who robbed me of my child! I'll cut his throat
and then my pain may find its antidote!"
Now, as you know, it was his false belief
that Joseph's killer was a beast of prey —
and so these wicked plotters did connive
to seize a wolf they'd trapped along the way
which they bound and brought to him alive,
"Behold your son's assassin — he's to blame!"
But the wolf sat up and called him by his name.

JOSEPH
AND HIS BROTHERS

vi. The Words of the Wolf

"Jacob," he said "I have not seen thy son!
As the Lord liveth, who created me
and you, and all the world, I promise thee
the flesh of man is something that I shun!
Look closer to home to find the guilty one,
and loose my iron bonds and set me free,
for men surpass mere wolves for cruelty
and well they know the evil they have done."
So Jacob let the wolf depart in peace
to roam unhindered in the wilderness,
for surely God had pitied his distress
and sent the wolf to grant him some release
from the consuming grief to which he clung:
sweet consolation from a wild beast's tongue.

JOSEPH
AND HIS BROTHERS

vii. The Cruel Secret

This is the part that's hardest to accept —
Jacob mourned for more than twenty years;
prostrate with grief, he shed a million tears
over that bloodstained cloak. Yet, while he wept
everyone in the family except
for Jacob knew the truth of the affair —
that Joseph was alive and well somewhere.
That was the cruel secret that they kept.
Grandfather Isaac surely must have known —
blessèd with the gift of prophecy;
to Jacob he expressed his sympathy,
but just as soon as he was quite alone
allowed himself to shake his head and smile,
remembering, perhaps, *his* father's trial.

JOSEPH
AND HIS BROTHERS

viii. Meanwhile in Egypt

The gift of prophecy deserts a seer
as long as he is in a state of grief
or lassitude. The soul requires belief
to see the present, past, and future clear,
and is struck blind by ennui or fear.
Passing of time brought Jacob no relief —
his visions left him, stolen by that thief
called sorrow — so it went for twenty years.
Meanwhile, in Egypt, Joseph's rise to power
as Pharaoh's trusted confidante and friend
set wheels in motion for the drama's end,
for God himself had fixed upon the hour
and setting of the fateful moment when
Joseph and his brothers meet again.

THE REUNION

JOSEPH WAS ONLY SEVENTEEN when he was sold into slavery by his brothers. First he won the favor of his master, Potiphar, who made him the steward of all his household.

Then, he won the favor of Pharaoh himself, by interpreting his dream as predicting seven years of plenty followed by seven years of famine.

Impressed, Pharaoh made Joseph governor of all of Egypt, and he filled the storehouses of the kingdom with grain.

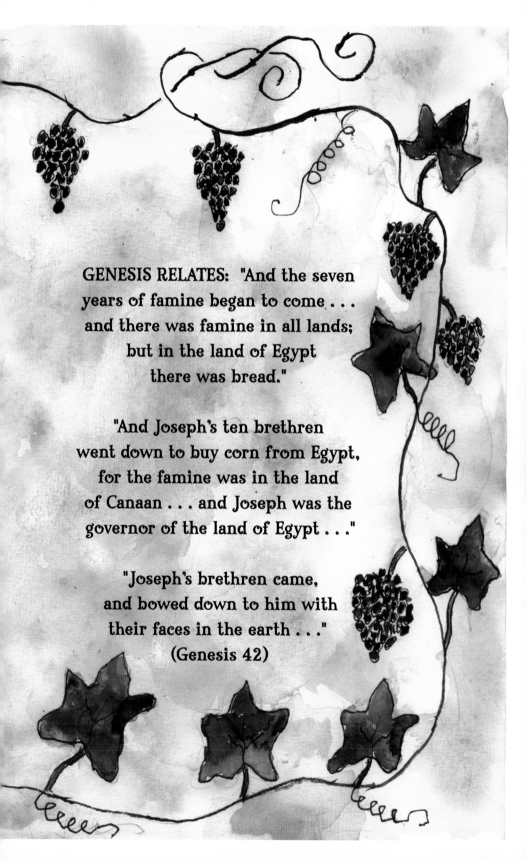

GENESIS RELATES: "And the seven
years of famine began to come . . .
and there was famine in all lands;
but in the land of Egypt
there was bread."

"And Joseph's ten brethren
went down to buy corn from Egypt,
for the famine was in the land
of Canaan . . . and Joseph was the
governor of the land of Egypt . . ."

"Joseph's brethren came,
and bowed down to him with
their faces in the earth . . ."
(Genesis 42)

THE REUNION

i. The Ten Brothers

Joseph knew his brothers right away —
In twenty years they hadn't changed that much —
Simon, eyeing enviously the plush
trappings of Pharaoh's palace; Dan blasé,
Gad with an air of boyish naiveté;
Zebulon anxious, always in a rush;
Reuben somber, lacking the common touch;
Judah, quick-witted, with a lot to say.
But his brothers knew not Joseph in disguise,
they marveled at his curiosity
about their far-off home and family,
"How do I know," he asked, "that you're not spies?"
"Nay, we are one man's sons," bold Levi said,
"we only journeyed here to purchase bread."

THE REUNION

ii. The Youngest Brother

"One man's sons? How many brothers, then?"
"Sire, we are twelve, from Jacob's wives and maids."
"How is it that I only count to ten?
Where are your brothers — somewhere making raids
on Egypt's borders? And will you come again
leading an army ready to blockade
our sleeping city?" "Nay, we're honest men;
one brother has been missing for decades;
the youngest is our father's only joy —
to lose this son would be to lose a limb,
so Benjamin remained at home with him."
Then Joseph's soul cried out to see the boy —
"Perhaps you lie, I need a guarantee —
go bring this youngest brother unto me."

THE REUNION

iii. The Souvenir

Now Benjamin had been a baby when
Joseph was kidnapped into servitude,
the only brother out of Jacob's brood
who played no part in all that happened then.
And furthermore, six of the other ten
were Leah's children, and so their attitude
was colored by the long domestic feud
between the sisters. Only Benjamin
remained a souvenir of Rachel's life.
Rachel had died in giving him his birth
and so, in Jacob's heart, this child was worth
the cost — the death of his beloved wife.
But Joseph yearned to hold his little brother
and see in him the lineaments of their mother.

THE REUNION

iv. Bad News

"Of *all* my children must I be bereaved?"
cried Jacob when they came back with the news.
"Simon a hostage, not allowed to leave;
Joseph missing, or dead *(though I accuse
no one!)*. Have I not already grieved
enough? If I must also lose
my Benjamin, the son that I conceived
in my old age, the grave is what I choose."
But the harvest withered under a burning sun —
with women and children starving in the lanes
Jacob knew that Canaan must have grain
or all would die. "Go now, take my last son,"
he said at last, "if I am left alone,
it is God's will, and so must be my own."

THE REUNION

v. A Day of Celebration

"These visitors shall dine with me at noon,"
said Joseph to his steward, "plan a feast,
invite them in, and do not spare the least
comfort—they shall dine on silver spoons,
and let the hall be festive, with festoons
of flowers. Take great care that all the meat
is ritually slaughtered, fit for Jews to eat;
make sure the harps and cymbals are in tune
for this will be a day of celebration,
laughter, and joy, but I will have some fun
with these petitioners before I'm done,
and there may be some sort of confrontation."
When Joseph's brothers saw the feast laid out
for them, they wondered, "What's this all about?"

THE REUNION

vi. That Old Man

"Your father, that old man of whom we spoke —
does he still live? And is he feeling well?"
Joseph asked his brothers. "And, pray tell,
who is that young man dressed up in a cloak
of many colors? Pardon me, the smoke
from all these cook stoves makes my eyelids swell!
Excuse me for a moment, while I quell
this malady," so Joseph sought to choke
back tears, and, looking for a place to weep
entered his room, and wept there for awhile;
and then he washed his face and with a smile
rejoined the group. "Tonight you all shall sleep
here in my house, tomorrow you shall be
homeward bound; come Benjamin, sit by me."

THE REUNION

vii. Proof of Robbery

When morning came he sent them on their way,
laden with food, as much as they could carry,
with admonitions that they should not tarry.
"In Canaan men are dying every day
of hunger, so there should be no delay."
But then he whispered to his young equerry
"Quickly, begone, ride after them, and hurry!
Stop them, and ask them 'Why do you betray
my master's kindliness by treachery?'
Then dump out Benjamin's sack, and you will find
my silver goblet, well concealed behind
his dirty laundry, proof of robbery.
Then say, 'Young man, it's useless to deny —
for this betrayal you must surely die!'"

THE REUNION

viii. One Last Chance

Now all of this was part of Joseph's dream
to give his faithless brothers one last chance
to prove their loyalty and take a stance
defending Benjamin, and thus redeem
their honor from the misbegotten scheme
of long ago. And, just as Joseph planned,
Judah begged "If this offense demands
a human life, slay me, and let it seem
my misdeed — lest my father's heart should break
and I must bear the blame forever more.
I promised him that I would die before
I let harm come to Benjamin. For his sake
send the boy home to him, and let me stay
to be thy servant till my dying day."

THE REUNION

ix. Come Closer

Then Joseph could no longer keep his tears
from flowing. He descended from the throne
and told his servants "Leave us now alone —
what I must say is not meant for your ears."
And thus no stranger stood with them to hear
when Joseph, weeping, made his story known
to his brothers, saying "Behold your own
brother Joseph, after all these years."
And then he said, "Come closer, have no fear
of me, I really am your brother;
and be not grieved, or angry with each other,
for it was God, not you, who sent me here
to Egypt, that a remnant might survive
the famine years, to keep us all alive."

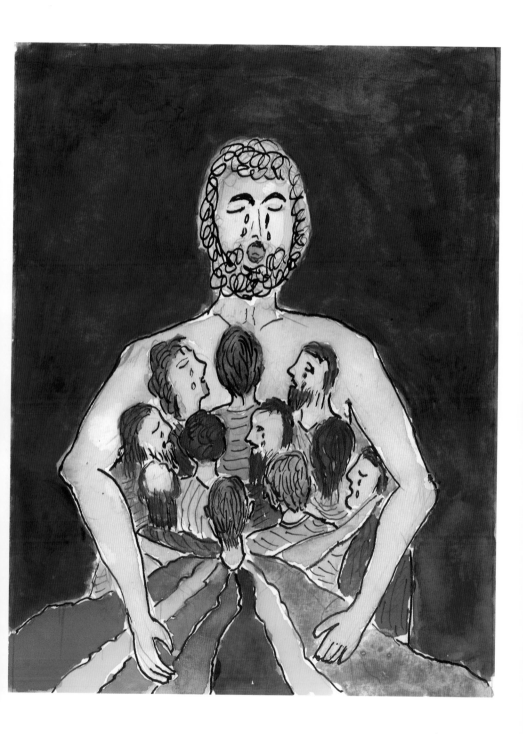

THE REUNION

x. Sudden Joy

With merry spirits on the following day
Joseph's kin began the journey back
to Canaan. Every bag and gunnysack
bulged with a splendiferous display
of gifts from Pharaoh, and all along the way
the common people stood along the track
and welcomed them at every bivouac
with feasting, song, and laughter. But the gay
mood faded when they reached the boundary line
of Canaan, and they said, "What shall we do
about our father? We had best contrive
a way to tell him Joseph is alive
that doesn't strike him right out of the blue,
for Joseph warned 'Take care you don't destroy
our father with the shock of sudden joy.'"

THE REUNION

xi. The Sound of Music

While they debated how to break the news
to Jacob, they were startled by the sound
of music. When they stopped to look around
a lovely maiden came into their view,
carrying a harp, as if on cue —
Serah, Asher's daughter, a renowned
harpist and singer. And thus they found
the instrument to carry out a ruse
designed to melt their father's shriveled heart
(hardened and deadened by his long distress)
and open it once more to happiness
by means of music's strong but simple art.
"Tonight," they told her, "sing as do the birds
in Jacob's ear, but we shall write the words."

THE REUNION

xii. Serah's Song

After dinner, when the plates were cleared,
the servants and the camels had been fed
and all the children hustled off to bed,
Serah raised her harp and volunteered
to play and sing a song for her revered
grandfather, Jacob, just as her uncles said.
"Joseph is alive, he is not dead!"
she sang, and, as she sang his vision cleared
and the gift of prophecy awoke in him
as dazzling as it had been in his youth,
and he understood that Serah sang the truth —
he saw it all, although his eyes were dim.
He cried out, "Joseph lives, that is no lie!
and I will see my son before I die."

THE REUNION

xiii. Shalom!

Then Benjamin, who'd been hiding in disguise,
burst in, exclaiming, "Father! Look! we're home!
We have seen Joseph, and he says 'Shalom!'
He sends his love, and begs you to arise
and come to him, for Pharaoh now denies
him nothing, and has set him on a throne
to govern all of Egypt. Joseph alone
decides who fills his belly and who dies.
But we must hurry, for there still remain
five years of famine, hunger, and starvation,
and it shall mean the death of many a nation,
but Joseph promised us 'I will sustain
your children through the years of poverty,
and they will dwell in Egypt, close to me.'"

THE REUNION

xiv. Visions of the Night

Then God spoke in the visions of the night
to Jacob, and He told him, "Do not fear
to go to Egypt, for I will take you there
Myself, and will protect you with My might,
and in the future, when the time is right
I'll bring you home again. So shed no tear
but take your families and all your gear —
load up the wagons, let your hearts be light
for I have plans to make a mighty nation
of Israel. Though there will be tough times
ahead for you, and slavery, and crimes
against your children, you will find salvation
and enter once again, with hope and glory
the promised land — but that's another story."

SARAH LAUGHED: Sonnets from Genesis is the second collaboration between poet Judith Goldhaber and artist Gerson Goldhaber, a husband-and-wife team from Berkeley, California. Their first book, *Sonnets from Aesop* (Ribbonweed Press) won the Independent Publishers Book Award (IPPY) as one of the ten best books published by an independent or university press in 2005.

JUDITH GOLDHABER is a poet, playwright, science writer, and journalist. Her poems have appeared in the National Poetry Review, The Garfield Lake Review, Prism, the Jewish Quarterly, Astropoetica, the Literary Review, and Byline. She is the recipient of numerous awards, including the Anna Davidson Rosenberg Award for Poems on the Jewish Experience, the National Poetry Review's Annie Finch Prize, and the "In the Beginning was the Word" poetry contest (in two consecutive years). As a playwright, she has written the book and lyrics for two musicals based on the lives of great individuals in modern science. Her musical about Stephen Hawking, Falling Through a Hole in the Air, received a $5,000 grant from Paul Newman's "Newman's Own" Foundation. and won a prize in the "Songs Judged as Poetry" of the National Poetry Association. Her newest musical is about Einstein's "lost" daughter Lieserl.

GERSON GOLDHABER is professor of physics in the graduate school at the University of California, Berkeley, and an artist who has worked in many media. His previous publications have been in the field of experimental particle physics and astrophysics. He is co-author of Experimental Foundations of Particle Physics (Cambridge University Press), and has written or co-authored over 250 papers reporting his research on elementary particles and cosmology. He is a member of the U.S. National Academy of Sciences, a fellow of the American Academy of Arts and Sciences, a Guggenheim fellow, and a foreign member of the Royal Swedish Academy of Sciences. He was named California Scientist of the Year in 1977, and is a winner of the Panofsky Prize of the American Physical Society.

SONNETS FROM AESOP

By Judith Goldhaber
Illustrations by Gerson Goldhaber

Winner of the Independent Publisher "Outstanding Book of the Year" Award

Aesop's timeless tales of outfoxed foxes, hapless lions, frisky donkeys, mutinous rabbits, wise insects, exasperated goddesses, and bewildered mortals are brought to new and vivid life in this collection of 100 sonnets by Judith Goldhaber, with watercolor illustrations by Gerson Goldhaber. Every generation needs to rediscover Aesop; here's a charming and readable delight for adults and children alike, equally suitable for coffee-table browsing or, as Aesop's Gluttonous Fox might prefer, devouring in one big gulp.

PRAISE FOR °SONNETS FROM AESOP°

"Judith Goldhaber has made wonderful new versions of Aesop's ancient fables. She is a virtuoso at rhyme and her use of the sonnet form to retell these stories preserves the traditional brevity of the originals. The result is irresistible, funny and wise . . . It surely should be the definitive Aesop for our day." – Craig Hill, author, *Beasts and Citizens* (translations from LaFontaine)

"To all readers, young and old, I commend these graceful and witty renditions of Aesop by Judith Goldhaber. And equally I recommend the playfully saturated, wry illustrations that accompany them. The only sour grapes for a reader will come if he or she leaves the book on the shelf!" — Roger Lathbury, Publisher, Orchises Press; Professor of English, George Mason University.

"What more could Aesop have wished than to address the 21st century in these dry, whimsical sonnets complemented by a series of soft, edgy watercolors? This beautifully produced book is a rare treat." — Annie Finch, poet, *Calendars* (shortlisted for the Foreword Poetry Book of the Year Award); Director, Stonecoast Low-Residency MFA, University of Southern Maine.

What a wonderful surprise! A local couple, writer and artist, worked together to create it . . What a great combination! This is an impressive book! — Reverend Gregory I. Carlson, S.J., Curator, Carlson Fables Collection at Creighton University.

Sonnets from Aesop is one of the most exciting works I've seen . . . Bottom line: buy this book. Buy one for your kids. Buy one for your neighbors' kids. Buy one for your nephews and nieces. Buy one for your public library—and the libraries of your local schools. — R. David Skinner, in Prism Quarterly

ISBN 0-9761554-0-0
Library of Congress Control Number: 2004097118
Ribbonweed Press, Berkeley, CA 94708-1402
Sonnets from Aesop is available on Amazon, Barnes & Noble, in many local bookstores, and at www.sonnetsfromaesop.com